This book belongs to:

If found, please do one good deed today
and return to:

....

One Good Deed a Day

One GOOD DEED A DAY

a journal

CHRONICLE BOOKS
SAN FRANCISCO

ISBN: 978-1-4521-0668-7

Manufactured in China

MIX
Paper from
responsible sources
FSC® C016973

Designed by **AYAKO AKAZAWA**
Illustrated by **KATIE DAISY**

10 9 8 7 6 5 4 3 2

CHRONICLE BOOKS LLC
680 Second Street
San Francisco, California 94107
www.chroniclebooks.com

*This book could not have been created without
the thoughtful contributions of*

Ayako Akazawa, Christina Amini, Laura Bagnato,
Sarah Billingsley, Mia Blankensop, Michelle Clair,
Catherine Cole, Jenna Cushner, Albee Dalbotten,
Sandy Davis, Guinevere de la Mare, Emily Dubin,
Julie Hamilton, Holden Hardcastle, Kristen Hewitt,
Brooke Johnson, Jennifer Kong, Kerri Kyle, Suzanne LaGasa,
Ben Laramie, Laura Lee Mattingly, Alyson Pullman,
Ariel Richardson, Kim Romero, Lindsay Sablosky,
Jason Sacher, Leigh Saffold, Emilie Sandoz, Jenifer Savasta,
Shannon Sawtelle, Sara Schneider, Lisa Tauber,
Jen Tolo Pierce, Amy Treadwell, Jodi Warshaw,
Bridget Watson Payne, Beth Weber, April Whitney,
Sarah Williams, Lorraine Woodcheke, Kate Woodrow,
Susan Woodrow, *and* Lynda Zuber Sassi.

Introduction

Kindness

is

contagious.

Consciously appreciating yourself, doing a favor for another—these are small actions that have great impact. And this journal offers 365 of them. Enough suggestions to infuse an entire year with extraordinary (and ordinary) compassion. As well as room to write and record ideas of your own.

Not sure where to start? Flip through the pages and choose whatever action speaks most to you today. Maybe you're motivated to prioritize your health and finally schedule that annual physical. Or perhaps your focus is on others today, and you choose to walk around your block picking up trash or call your parents to tell them what you appreciate most about them. All the actions in this journal are manageable enough to be accomplished in a day. And each one of these seemingly simple measures has the power to set off a chain reaction of kindness. Good deeds never go unnoticed. In fact, they tend to have a ripple effect. Your kind smile can compel someone to hold the door for a stranger, motivating that stranger to reach out to an old friend, who decides to donate much-needed funds to a charitable cause.

Wherever you choose to start, commit to completing that action before the day is through, and mark your page with the ribbon marker. Take a moment to notice the effect your good deed has—on you, on the people you love, or on complete strangers. When you get home, check it off with the date of completion and jot down some notes about what you did. What reactions did you get? How did doing that good deed make you feel? Would you ever do it again? By journaling, even just a line or two, you'll solidify that fleeting moment of satisfaction our good deeds deliver. And perhaps, upon reflection, you'll be motivated to do another good deed tomorrow, and the next day, and the next . . .

Smile
at a
stranger.

reflect: _____

_____

_____

Become an organ donor.

reflect:

Add money to an expired meter.

reflect:

Talk about what you're grateful for.

reflect: _____

_____

_____

Walk around your block and

Pick up
some trash.

reflect: _____

_____

_____

Be kind
to
yourself.

reflect: _____

_____

_____

Send
one of your
grandparents
a photograph.

reflect: _____

_____

_____

Forgive
someone

for a minor resentment
that's been bothering you.

reflect:

_____

_____

_____

Send a friend
a beloved book

from your shelf.

reflect:

Choose
the longer walk
home.

reflect:
_____
_____
_____

Take your neighbor's trash bins in

off the curb.

reflect:

Treat
yourself.

reflect: _____

_____

_____

Leave your change

in the vending machine
for the next person.

reflect:

_____

_____

_____

Give yourself a pep talk.

reflect:
_____

_____

_____

Hold the elevator door

even if it will delay you.

reflect:

Spend
no money
today.

reflect:

Start a list of books you'd like to

Read
for fun.

reflect: _____

_____

_____

Eat your next meal in silence

(away from a computer).

reflect: _____

_____

_____

Strike up a conversation

with the person working the cash register.

reflect: _____

_____

_____

Serve food
at a
food bank.

reflect:
_____

_____

_____

Visit your local library.

reflect:

Tell a friend she's beautiful.

reflect: _____

_____

_____

Say hello
to strangers,

especially to the elderly.

reflect: _____

_____

_____

Pay for someone behind you

at the lunch counter.

reflect: _____

_____

_____

Ask a friend who seems down to

Go for
a walk.

reflect:

Be
mindful

of saying "Please" and "Thank-you" and "You're welcome"
—all day long.

reflect: _____

_____

_____

Be quick
to apologize.

reflect:

Find
ways to help
others

avoid embarrassment.

reflect:
_____
_____
_____

Volunteer

at an elder care facility.

reflect: _____

_____

_____

Allow everyone else to go first

all day.

reflect:
_____
_____
_____

Deliver something small and sweet

to everyone on your team—midafternoon, just when everyone's energy wanes.

reflect: _____

_____

_____

Stand on the corner with a sign that says,

"You are perfect."

reflect: _____

_____

_____

Put a love note in a loved one's lunch.

reflect: _____

_____

_____

Invite a friend to dinner,

but bring it to him at his house. Then clean up.

reflect:

Buy a
bunch of
flowers

on your way to work. Give each one to a colleague you appreciate.

reflect: _____

_____

_____

Tell your parents you love them

and appreciate them.

reflect: _____

_____

_____

Drop
a meal off

at a sick friend's house.

reflect: _____

_____

_____

Donate blood.

reflect: _____

_____

_____

Record
a message
or video

and send to one of your grandparents.

reflect:

_____

_____

_____

Be happy for somebody

and tell her.

reflect:

_____

_____

_____

COMPLETED ON

_____

DATE

Clean out your sweater drawer and

Take extras to a charity.

reflect: _____

_____

_____

Send a friend a thank-you note

for being a good friend.

reflect: _____

_____

_____

Take a sibling out to a movie.

reflect: _____

_____

_____

Let another car take that parking spot.

Smile and wave.

reflect: _____

_____

_____

Tell a stranger his child is beautiful.

reflect: _____

_____

_____

Give up
your seat

on the bus or train for someone who seems tired.

reflect:

Smile at kids

or give them a silly face to distract them and
give their parents a moment of reprieve.

reflect:

Visit
an animal
shelter.

reflect: _____

_____

_____

Learn your local barista's name and use it.

reflect: _____

_____

_____

Give credit wherever you can.

reflect: _____

_____

_____

Hug
your child
for no reason
at all.

reflect: _____

_____

_____

Send a handwritten thank-you note.

reflect: _____

_____

_____

Call
your mother

and tell her something you loved about being her kid.

reflect: _____

_____

_____

Write a postcard to a long-lost friend.

reflect:

Do a little dance and be silly.

reflect:
_____
_____
_____

Pick up
the tab.

reflect:

Bake your favorite kind of cookies, and

Share.

reflect: _____

_____

_____

Shovel
the snow

off your neighbor's porch.

reflect: _____

_____

_____

Tell the people you love, "I love you."

reflect:

Buy a coffee

for the person behind you in line.

reflect: _____

_____

_____

Fill
the printer
with paper

so it won't run out on the next person.

reflect:

_____

_____

_____

Don't eat meat today.

reflect:
_____
_____
_____

Take your dad out for lunch.

reflect:

Offer
to babysit

so new parents can go out to dinner.

reflect: _____

_____

_____

Print and frame
a good picture

you've taken of someoné and give it to him.

reflect:

Meditate
for
ten minutes.

reflect: _____

_____

_____

Write a
list of things

you're grateful for.

reflect: _____

_____

_____

Bring
your neighbor's
newspaper

to her doorstep.

reflect: _____

_____

_____

Bless your interruptions as an opportunity to

Take a deep breath and smile.

reflect: _____

_____

_____

Run a little fund-raiser

(a clothing exchange, a bake sale)
for someone who is struggling with an expense.

reflect:

Send your mom flowers

for no reason.

reflect: _____

_____

_____

Donate
to a
charity

that benefits animals or children.

reflect: _____

_____

_____

Smile
when you
talk on
the phone

—it makes your voice friendly.

reflect:

Buy a nice water bottle,

so you'll be less inclined to buy plastic bottles.

reflect:

Kiss
the cook.

reflect:
_____
_____
_____

Leave some homemade cookies

at your neighbor's door.

reflect:

Give a homeless person a clean blanket.

reflect: _____

_____

_____

Return a long-overdue phone call.

reflect: _____

_____

_____

Compliment a complete stranger.

reflect: _____

_____

_____

Sneak
a note into a
friend's purse,

wallet, or drawer for her to discover later.

reflect: _____

_____

_____

Write a letter to someone

who has changed your life and might not even know it.

reflect: _____

_____

_____

Bake with your kids.

reflect:

Start a recycling program

at your building, school, or home.

reflect: _____

_____

_____

Pack a spontaneous picnic

and go outside with your family.

reflect: _____

_____

_____

Invite
your neighbor
to dinner.

reflect:

Tell a stranger he is being a good parent.

reflect: _____

_____

_____

COMPLETED ON

_____

DATE

Ask your Twitter followers or Facebook friends
if there's anything you can do to

Support them right now.

reflect: _____

_____

_____

Hold the door open for someone.

reflect: _____

_____

_____

Call someone in your family just to

Tell him you're thinking about him.

reflect: _____

_____

_____

Start
a birthday
calendar

to help you remember to mail cards.

reflect: _____

_____

_____

Take out
the garbage,

without being asked.

reflect: _____

_____

_____

Leave
a big tip.

reflect: _____

_____

_____

Bring
your coworker
a coffee.

reflect:

Take your partner out to lunch

on a workday.

reflect:

Leave your mail carrier a thank-you note

for delivering your mail every week.

reflect:

When someone does or says something rude or offensive,
assume she is having a bad day and

Respond with compassion.

reflect:

Mail homemade cookies to a friend.

reflect:

Wave hello

at a four-way stop, yielding to the other person.

reflect: _____

_____

_____

Have a glass of wine ready for your spouse

when he or she arrives home from work.

reflect: _____

_____

_____

Wish
your cashier a
good day.

reflect: _____

_____

_____

Prank call
a friend

when you know he is bored.

reflect:

Plant a seed.

reflect: _____

_____

_____

Apologize

to someone you've wronged.

reflect: _____

_____

_____

Thank your
bus driver

for delivering you safely to your destination.

reflect: _____

_____

_____

COMPLETED ON

_____

DATE

Say "I love you"

to someone you haven't said it to in a while.

reflect: _____

_____

_____

Play hooky.

reflect:
_____

_____

_____

Tell a family member why you appreciate her.

reflect:

Donate
a little bit of
money

to aid disaster-relief work somewhere in the world.

reflect:
_____
_____
_____

Listen.

reflect: _____

_____

_____

Leave a favorite book on a bus

or train seat for the next passenger to enjoy.

reflect: _____

_____

_____

Cook dinner for your roommate,

neighbor, or friend.

reflect:

Send a note to a favorite teacher

telling him the best thing he taught you.

reflect:

Send an uplifting note to a friend

to a friend

who might need encouragement.

reflect: _____

_____

_____

Reward yourself.

reflect: _____

_____

_____

Teach a kid
a funny joke.

reflect: _____

_____

_____

Scroll through your phone and

Call the person you've known the longest.

reflect:

Play freeze
dance.

reflect:

Be the first
to apologize.

reflect:

Mow your neighbor's grass

along with your own.

reflect:
_____
_____
_____

Read more

about a cause that you are interested in.

reflect: _____

_____

_____

Instead of ignoring someone's pain
because you don't know what to say,

Send a small gift card.

reflect:

_____

_____

_____

Make a baby laugh.

reflect: _____

_____

_____

Tuck your
sweetheart in.

reflect:

Stop
swearing.

reflect:

Volunteer.

reflect:

Take a yoga class.

reflect: _____

_____

_____

Schedule your annual physical.

reflect:

Say something nice

to someone who's wronged you.

reflect:

_____

_____

_____

Set high expectations.

reflect: _____

_____

_____

Make time to

Visit an
art museum.

reflect:
_____

_____

_____

Give an anonymous donation

to a person or family in need.

reflect: _____

_____

_____

Listen to
your heart.

reflect:

Learn how to change a tire

so you can do it yourself or
someday help out a stranger in need.

reflect: _____

_____

_____

COMPLETED ON

DATE

Go for a swim.

reflect:

Pray
for others.

reflect:
_____
_____
_____

Swap
life stories

with someone you don't know very well.

reflect: _____

_____

_____

Thank your trash collectors

and tell them they're doing a good job.

reflect:

Write a nice little note

on the check to your server.

reflect: _____

_____

_____

Offer a glass
of water

to the meter reader, appliance repairman, or
delivery person at your home.

reflect:

Write a song for someone.

reflect: _____

_____

_____

Return all of the items

you take into the dressing room to their original spots
instead of leaving them in the dressing room.

reflect: _____

_____

_____

Let a stranger know if a button is undone

or she has lipstick on her teeth.

reflect:

_____

_____

_____

Send
a card
to a coach
or boss

to whom you are grateful.

reflect: _____

_____

_____

Recognize
your coworker

or teammate for something difficult or daunting
he is working on.

reflect: _____

_____

_____

Invite an acquaintance out for coffee.

reflect:

Send a card
and seeds
to a neighbor

whose garden you admire.

reflect:

Say
good morning
to your
coworkers.

reflect:

Look someone in the eyes and

Thank her sincerely.

reflect: _____

_____

_____

Stop and
pet a dog

and say hello to the owner.

reflect: _____

_____

_____

Tell someone he is appreciated.

reflect: _____

_____

_____

Leave someone a handwritten note

to "have a good day."

reflect:

_____

_____

_____

Compliment someone's new haircut

or shoes or hat, etc.

reflect: _____

_____

_____

Make a really fancy and complicated dessert,

and deliver it to a friend as a surprise.

reflect: _____

_____

_____

Set
the road rage
aside,

and let someone else merge.

reflect:

Acknowledge others' kindness

with a smile or a wave.

reflect: _____

_____

_____

Do or say something funny

that's sure to make a friend laugh.

reflect: _____

_____

_____

Share some good news.

reflect: _____

_____

_____

Offer to do someone a favor.

reflect:

Send a sibling a reminder of childhood.

reflect:

Accept that good is good enough.

reflect: _____

_____

_____

Say "Gesundheit"

when a stranger sneezes.

reflect: _____

_____

_____

Ask someone what's bothering her,

and then listen.

reflect: _____

_____

_____

Empty the dishwasher

before anyone in your house or office
has a chance to ask you to do it.

reflect: _____

_____

_____

Establish
an emergency
plan

with your family or friends.

reflect: _____

_____

_____

Hide
some money in
the pocket
of a coat

that's for sale.

reflect: _____

_____

_____

Clean up someone else's mess.

reflect: _____

_____

_____

Tape a coupon to a product

at the grocery store.

reflect: _____

_____

_____

Pay for
a stranger's
meal

at a restaurant.

reflect:

Establish
a tradition.

reflect: _____

_____

_____

Turn
your telephone
ringer off,

and appreciate some uninterrupted moments.

reflect: _____

_____

_____

Buy a plant
for your desk.

reflect: _____

_____

_____

Figure out how to

Print
double-sided.

reflect:

_____

_____

_____

Think big, and then think bigger.

reflect: _____

_____

_____

Accept and enjoy yourself

for who you are.

reflect: _____

_____

_____

Tell a joke.

reflect:

Forget
everything

else and focus on falling asleep.

reflect:

Raise your arms high above your head and

Stretch the biggest stretch you can stretch.

reflect:
_____
_____
_____

Choose a glass of water

instead of another coffee.

reflect: _____

_____

_____

Take off your cranky pants.

reflect:

Wait a beat before responding.

reflect: _____

_____

_____

Listen
to a radio
program

while doing nothing else at the same time.

reflect:

Write down everything on your mind.

Take a step back so you can take a fresh look.

reflect: _____

_____

_____

Ask your partner about his day.

Listen.

reflect:

Take a walk,

looking as far in the distance as possible.

reflect: _____

_____

_____

Give someone a wink.

reflect:

Find a book
on tape

or a podcast that will amuse you while you commute.

reflect:

Put yourself first.

reflect: _____

_____

_____

Donate books

to a local school or university.

reflect: _____

_____

_____

Tell a relative what you admire about him.

reflect: _____

_____

_____

Share a family recipe.

reflect: _____

_____

_____

Make up your own family holiday to celebrate.

reflect:

Donate your ponytail after a haircut.

reflect: _____

_____

_____

Write a letter

to a politician —about something she is doing right.

reflect: _____

_____

_____

Learn about a new country or culture.

reflect: _____

_____

_____

COMPLETED ON

DATE

Ask
your partner

about what she wants to conquer next.

reflect:

Join a team.

reflect:

Leave a
nice comment

on your friend's blog, Facebook wall, or Twitter feed.

reflect: _____

_____

_____

Buy a present

for a friend's beloved pet.

reflect:
_____

_____

_____

Offer
to give your
loved one
a massage.

reflect:

Borrow someone's car and get it cleaned.

reflect:

Create a scrapbook of memories

for your family or friends.

reflect: _____
_____
_____

Write
a poem for
someone.

reflect:

Give someone one piece of constructive criticism.

reflect:

Tell a friend why he means the world to you.

reflect: _____

_____

_____

Make
a donation

to a friend's favorite charity in her name.

reflect:

Hang
a bird feeder

to support the local avian population.

reflect:

Tuck an origami heart into the windowsill

of a bus for someone to find later.

reflect:

Draw a hopscotch grid on the sidewalk,
and watch how people will

Enjoy feeling like kids again.

reflect: _____

_____

_____

Sign up
for a run

or a walk that supports a special cause.

reflect: _____

_____

_____

Say hello
to a stranger.

reflect: _____

_____

_____

Sneak over to a friend's house and

Plant bulbs to surprise her next spring.

reflect: _____

_____

_____

Have a lights-free day,

complete with candles at night.

reflect:

_____

_____

_____

Line dry your laundry

instead of using the dryer.

reflect: _____

_____

_____

Accept a new friend's invitation.

reflect:

Recycle.

reflect: _____

_____

_____

Don't double-book yourself.

reflect:

Visit a community garden.

reflect:
_____

_____

_____

Refrain from talking loudly

on your cell phone in public.

reflect:

Bring
your own bags
to the store.

reflect:

Designate yourself an ambassador

to your town and vow to offer directions
to anyone who looks a little lost.

reflect:

Say a blessing out loud

for one thing you are grateful for.

reflect:
_____

_____

_____

Call your busiest friend and insist on helping

with one thing he needs to get done.

reflect: _____

_____

_____

Donate old eyeglasses.

reflect:

Say yes.

reflect: _____

_____

_____

Dress fancy

or with a flourish today. Turn heads.

reflect:

Encourage a colleague to

Take some much-needed time off.

reflect:

Stop and
look around.

reflect:

Take an unpopular

Stand for something you believe in.

reflect: _____

_____

_____

Ask your grandparents

about favorite trips they've taken or places they've lived.

reflect: _____

_____

_____

Compliment

someone over seventy.

reflect: _____

_____

_____

Teach a child five new words.

reflect: _____

_____

_____

Leave
flowers
for a stranger.

reflect: _____

_____

_____

Offer to go on a walk

with a stressed friend.

reflect:

Buy someone an ice cream cone.

reflect:

Carry a bunch of balloons.

Watch heads turn.

reflect: _____

_____

_____

Go to an independent

(bookstore, movie, or business).

reflect: _____

_____

_____

Organize a clothing swap.

reflect:

_____

_____

_____

Carpool.

reflect: _____

_____

_____

Listen to a solicitor's whole pitch

(even if you're planning to say "no").

reflect:
_____

_____

_____

Make an effort to

Mend a rift
in a friendship.

reflect:

Make art.

reflect:

Don't interrupt anyone today.

reflect: _____

_____

_____

Stop
obsessing

over someone who's wronged you.

reflect: _____

_____

_____

Give

money

to a street performer.

reflect: _____

_____

_____

Teach
someone one
of your skills.

reflect:

Withhold
judgment

until the end of the sentence.

reflect:

Take a long bath.

reflect: _____

_____

_____

Call

someone

to tell her you were thinking about her.

reflect:
_____

_____

_____

See
all you can
see.

reflect:

Play a song you love

as loudly as you want.

reflect:

Give people the benefit of the doubt.

reflect:

Pay for
the car
behind you

at the toll booth.

reflect: _____

_____

_____

Buy organic.

reflect:
_____

_____

_____

Lend someone an article of clothing

they've admired.

reflect:

_____

_____

_____

Bag your own groceries.

reflect:

_____

_____

_____

Change your lightbulbs

to compact fluorescent lightbulbs (CFLs).

reflect: _____

_____

_____

Make a handmade card for someone.

reflect:

Let it go.

reflect:
_____

_____

_____

Tell your colleague he is brilliant!

reflect:

_____

_____

_____

Make someone laugh.

reflect: _____

_____

_____

If you're thinking about donating money,
ask a friend to contribute and

Increase
the impact.

reflect: _____

_____

_____

Tell
your mom
one thing

she's always done right.

reflect: _____

_____

_____

Tell your dad about something

you're so glad he taught you.

reflect: _____

_____

_____

Make signs for the trash,

recycling, and compost so it's clear what goes where.

reflect: _____

_____

_____

Master a
family recipe.

reflect: _____
_____
_____

Help;
don't ignore.

reflect:
_____

_____

_____

Ride
your bike!

reflect:

Teach

someone

something about another culture.

reflect:

COMPLETED ON

_____

DATE

Buy
two books

—one for you and one for a friend.

reflect: _____

_____

_____

Hold
your tongue.

reflect:

Write a letter to your future self

and stash it away to discover later.

reflect: _____

_____

_____

Learn how to say "Thank you"

in other languages so you can thank
people in their native tongues.

reflect:

Frame a family photo,

and hang it on your wall.

reflect: _____

_____

_____

Carry a safety pin in your bag

—someone will be so grateful you have one.

reflect: _____

_____

_____

Quote your grandfather.

reflect:
_____

_____

_____

Tell
the story

of the person you are named after.

reflect: _____

_____

_____

Start a family tree.

reflect: _____

_____

_____

Buy a box of thank-you notes

and birthday cards so you're always ready to mark an occasion.

reflect:

Add a reminder to vote

in your calendar.

reflect:

Take your grandmother out

for a fancy cocktail.

reflect:

Volunteer
to read books

to little kids.

reflect:

Get some exercise.

reflect: _____

_____

_____

Pack
extra lunch

for a coworker.

reflect: _____

_____

_____

Plan a party.

Invite someone new.

reflect: _____

_____

_____

Take a deep breath.

Now take two more. Repeat.

reflect:

Experiment

with a vegan or vegetarian meal.

reflect: _____

_____

_____

Ask
"How are you?"

and really listen for more than "Fine."

reflect: _____

_____

_____

Thank someone for something

you usually take for granted.

reflect: _____

_____

_____

Spell-check and proofread

before you send.

reflect:

Turn off your cell phone.

reflect: _____

_____

_____

COMPLETED ON

DATE

Make a
special meal

for someone you love.

reflect:

Get some
fresh air.

reflect: _____

_____

_____

Leave a treat on your coworker's desk.

reflect:
_____
_____
_____

Buy double the canned goods and

Donate the extras at a food bank.

reflect: _____

_____

_____

Go to a friend's gallery opening,

sports game, poetry reading, play . . . finally.

reflect: _____

_____

_____

Wake up thirty minutes earlier

and get some exercise.

reflect:

Get a library card.

reflect:

Return
that book,

movie, or dish you borrowed from a friend...
three years ago.

reflect: _____

_____

_____

Make a
special treat

for a friend with food allergies.

reflect:

Laugh louder.

reflect: _____

_____

_____

Brew
the next pot
of coffee

at work or home.

reflect:

Write a letter

to an author you admire.

reflect:

Draw
a portrait of
a friend

(all the better if you have no drawing skills).

reflect: _____

_____

_____

Tip your barista.

reflect:

Wear something your mother gave you,

even if you hate it.

reflect: _____

_____

_____

Watch
the movie

that your significant other wants to watch.

reflect: _____

_____

_____

Add
a few
plants

to your bedroom.

reflect: _____

_____

_____

Close
your ears
to gossip

this week.

reflect: _____

_____

_____

Leave a bookmark

in a book you've borrowed.

reflect:
_____
_____
_____

Tell
parents

when their kids seem well behaved or smart or nice.

reflect: _____

_____

_____

Be a
mentor.

reflect:
_____

_____

_____

Start a composting program

at your building, school, or home.

reflect: _____

_____

_____

Tend to an elderly neighbor's garden.

reflect: _____

_____

_____

Be on time all day today.

reflect:

Exhale.

reflect: _____

_____

_____

Ask your mother for one of her favorite recipes.

reflect:

_____

_____

_____

Leave an umbrella in a public place

for someone to use.

reflect:

_____

_____

_____

Read
a classic.

reflect: _____

_____

_____

Drink
eight glasses
of water.

reflect:

_____

_____

_____

Unplug all the appliances

in your house that aren't being used.

reflect:

Buy lunch for a homeless person.

reflect: _____

_____

_____

Propose
a game.

reflect:

Encourage
somebody.

reflect: _____

_____

_____

Use a funny word,

like "wackadoodle" or "lollygag."

reflect: _____

_____

_____

Bring
extra coupons

to the store and share.

reflect: _____

_____

_____

Pay attention.

Invite a friend
to a show

and buy her ticket.

reflect: _____

_____

_____

Be honest,

especially when the truth is wonderful.

reflect: _____

_____

_____

When you are inspired to say something nice,

Say it.

reflect: _____

_____

_____

Offer
your respects,
always.

reflect: _____

_____

_____

Be understanding and truthful.

reflect: _____

_____

_____

Watch a classic movie

you've always wanted to see.

reflect: _____

_____

_____

Have
a meatless
Monday.

reflect: _____

_____

_____

Put a little cash in your savings account.

reflect:

Look and
listen.

Go out for coffee

with a coworker you don't know well.

reflect:

_____

_____

_____

Celebrate other people's successes.

reflect:

Don't take offense.

reflect: _____

_____

_____

Tell
your mom

your favorite memory of her.

reflect:
_____
_____
_____

Tell
your dad

your favorite memory of him.

reflect: _____

_____

_____

Smile at a meter maid.

reflect:

Foster a kitten
or puppy.

reflect:

Leave a bunch of extra change

near the jukebox, at the laundromat, or by the vending machine.

reflect:

Tell
your dentist

you appreciate him.

reflect: _____

_____

_____

COMPLETED ON

_____
DATE

Offer up
a foot rub.

reflect: _____
_____
_____

Knit or sew a gift for a new baby.

reflect:

COMPLETED ON

_____
DATE

Befriend
someone new.

reflect:

_____
_____
_____

Be a gentleman or gentlewoman.

reflect: _____

_____

_____

Buy
handmade.

reflect: _____

_____

_____

Recommend your favorite hole-in-the-wall

place to get food.

reflect:

Join or start a community garden.

reflect: _____

_____

_____

Invite someone to join you.

reflect: _____

_____

_____

Find out
how your
dad proposed

to your mom.

reflect: _____

_____

_____

Look
into the eyes

of the person you are talking with.

reflect:

Floss.

reflect: _____

_____

_____

Plant
flowers

where someone else will enjoy them.

reflect: _____

_____

_____

Offer
your car

to a friend without wheels.

reflect: _____
_____
_____

Make up a story

and tell it to a young person in your life.

reflect: _____

_____

_____

Keep your promises.

reflect: _____

_____

_____

Leave
flowers

on the statue of someone you admire.

reflect:

Tell someone he has beautiful eyes.

reflect:

Commit.

reflect: _____

_____

_____

COMPLETED ON

_____

DATE

Find two days this year when you can

Donate
your time.

reflect: _____

_____

_____

Plan a birthday party for a friend.

Make it memorable.

reflect:

Push the
boundaries.

reflect: _____

_____

_____

COMPLETED ON

_____

DATE

What else can you do?

reflect: _____

_____

_____

What else can you do?

reflect: _____
_____
_____

What else can you do?

reflect:

What else can you do?

reflect: _____

_____

_____

What else can you do?

reflect:

What else can you do?

reflect: _____
_____
_____

What else can you do?

reflect:

COMPLETED ON

_____

DATE

What else can you do?

reflect: _____

_____

_____

COMPLETED ON

DATE

What else can you do?

reflect:

What else can you do?

reflect: _____

_____

_____

What else can you do?

reflect:

_____

_____

_____

What else can you do?

reflect: _____

_____

_____

What else can you do?

reflect: _____

_____

_____

What else can you do?

reflect: _____

_____

_____